GRADE
3

Success With

Addition & Subtraction

SCHOLASTIC

Editor: Ourania Papacharalambous
Cover design by Tannaz Fassihi; cover illustration by Kevin Zimmer
Interior design by Mina Chen
Interior illustrations by Doug Jones (4); Kathy Marlin (5, 6, 16, 17, 30, 31, 38, 43, 44, 46); Pauline Reeves (22, 24, 25, 28)
All other images @ Shutterstock.com

ISBN 978-1-338-79830-2
Scholastic Inc., 557 Broadway, New York, NY 10012
Copyright © 2022 Scholastic Inc.
All rights reserved. Printed in the U.S.A.
First printing, January 2022
1 2 3 4 5 6 7 8 9 10   40   29 28 27 26 25 24 23 22

INTRODUCTION

Parents and teachers alike will find *Scholastic Success With Addition & Subtraction* to be a valuable educational tool. These practice pages incorporate challenging puzzles, inviting games, and picture problems that will both stimulate and encourage children as they improve their math skills. On page 4, you will find a list of the key skills covered in the activities throughout this book. Children are challenged to sharpen their addition and subtraction skills, solve word problems, and more. Remember to praise children for their efforts and successes!

TABLE OF CONTENTS

Key Skills **4**

Sails on the Ocean (*Add to 18*) **5**

Packing for an Expedition (*Subtract from 18*) **6**

Class Trip (*Add/Subtract through 18*) **7**

Let Freedom Ring
(*Add 2-digit numbers without regrouping*) **8**

The United States and Canada
(*Add/Subtract 2-digit numbers without regrouping*) **9**

Stars and Stripes (*Regrouping review—ones to tens*) **10**

The U.S. Capital
(*Add 2-digit numbers with regrouping*) **11**

American Presidents
(*Add 2-digit numbers with regrouping*) **12**

Time for a Trip! (*Regrouping review—tens to ones*) **13**

Great Vacations
(*Subtract 2-digit numbers with regrouping*) **14**

Weather in the United States
(*Subtract 2-digit numbers with regrouping*) **15**

Cooling Off
(*Subtract 2-digit numbers with regrouping*) **16**

America's Favorite Pastime
(*Add/Subtract 2-digit numbers with regrouping*) **17**

High-Scoring Game
(*Add/Subtract 2-digit numbers with regrouping*) **18**

More Fun Sports
(*Add/Subtract 2-digit numbers with regrouping*) **19**

Skating Shapes
(*Add/Subtract 2-digit numbers with regrouping*) **20**

Great Math Inventions
(*Add/Subtract 2-digit numbers with regrouping*) **21**

It All Adds Up!
(*Add 3-digit numbers without regrouping*) **22**

It's Electrifying!
(*Regrouping review—tens to hundreds*) **23**

Let the Light Shine
(*Regrouping review—hundreds to tens*) **24**

A, B, C . . . (*Add 3-digit numbers with regrouping*) **25**

. . . X, Y, and Z (*Add 3-digit numbers with regrouping*).. **26**

Number Decoder
(*Subtract 3-digit numbers with regrouping*) **27**

Out of This World
(*Subtract 3-digit numbers with regrouping*) **28**

Ride Through the Clouds
(*Add/Subtract 3-digit numbers with regrouping*) **29**

Mailbox Mix-Up
(*Add/Subtract 3-digit numbers with regrouping*) **30**

Your Part of the World
(*Add/Subtract 3-digit numbers with regrouping*) **31**

Home Sweet Home
(*Add/Subtract 3-digit numbers with regrouping*) **32**

What a Beautiful World!
(*Add/Subtract 3-digit numbers with regrouping*) **33**

Majestic Mountains
(*Add 4-digit numbers without regrouping*) **34**

Reach for the Top
(*Add 4-digit numbers without regrouping*) **35**

One in a Thousand
(*Add money/Regrouping review*) **36**

Did You Know?
(*Add/Subtract money with regrouping*) **37**

Great Beginnings
(*Add 4-digit numbers with regrouping*) **38**

Styles Change
(*Add 4-digit numbers with regrouping*) **39**

Dynamite Dominoes
(*Regrouping review—thousands to hundreds*) **40**

Pictures in the Sky
(*Subtract 4-digit numbers with regrouping*) **41**

Imaginary Lines
(*Add/Subtract 4-digit numbers with regrouping*) **42**

Long, Long Ago
(*Add/Subtract 4-digit numbers with regrouping*) **43**

Fun With Numbers
(*Add/Subtract 4-digit numbers with regrouping*) **44**

Classy Animals
(*Add/Subtract 4-digit numbers with regrouping*) **45**

Answer Key **46**

Grade-Appropriate Skills Covered in *Scholastic Success With Addition & Subtraction: Grade 3*

Add up to four two-digit numbers using strategies based on place value and properties of operations.

Solve two-step word problems using the four operations. Represent these problems using equations with a letter standing for the unknown quantity. Assess the reasonableness of answers using mental computation and estimation strategies including rounding.

Identify arithmetic patterns and explain them using properties of operations.

Use place value understanding to round whole numbers to the nearest 10 or 100.

Fluently add and subtract within 1,000, using strategies and algorithms based on place value, properties of operations, and/or the relationship between addition and subtraction.

Understand that the three digits of a three-digit number represent amounts of hundreds, tens, and ones.

Sails on the Ocean

Add.

Packing for an Expedition

Subtract. Then, use the code to write a letter for each difference to see what explorers might have packed for an expedition in the 1600s. Put an **X** on the item an explorer from the 1600s would not pack.

$$\begin{array}{r} 15 \\ -\ 1 \\ \hline \end{array} \qquad \begin{array}{r} 16 \\ -\ 8 \\ \hline \end{array} \qquad \begin{array}{r} 15 \\ -\ 13 \\ \hline \end{array} \qquad \begin{array}{r} 13 \\ -\ 8 \\ \hline \end{array} \qquad \begin{array}{r} 16 \\ -\ 5 \\ \hline \end{array} \qquad\qquad \begin{array}{r} 7 \\ -\ 5 \\ \hline \end{array} \qquad \begin{array}{r} 15 \\ -\ 8 \\ \hline \end{array} \qquad \begin{array}{r} 17 \\ -\ 6 \\ \hline \end{array}$$

◯ ◯ ◯ ◯ ◯   ◯ ◯ ◯

$$\begin{array}{r} 18 \\ -\ 14 \\ \hline \end{array} \qquad \begin{array}{r} 11 \\ -\ 9 \\ \hline \end{array} \qquad \begin{array}{r} 17 \\ -\ 12 \\ \hline \end{array} \qquad \begin{array}{r} 16 \\ -\ 15 \\ \hline \end{array} \qquad \begin{array}{r} 17 \\ -\ 0 \\ \hline \end{array}$$

◯ ◯ ◯ ◯ ◯

$$\begin{array}{r} 18 \\ -\ 4 \\ \hline \end{array} \qquad \begin{array}{r} 10 \\ -\ 8 \\ \hline \end{array} \qquad \begin{array}{r} 18 \\ -\ 8 \\ \hline \end{array} \qquad \begin{array}{r} 12 \\ -\ 1 \\ \hline \end{array} \qquad \begin{array}{r} 15 \\ -\ 11 \\ \hline \end{array}$$

◯ ◯ ◯ ◯ ◯

17	10	4	7	11	5	14	8	1	2
o	b	r	x	e	d	s	p	i	a

Class Trip

Add or subtract. Write the names in alphabetical order by sequencing the answers from greatest to smallest.

Pari	14 − 7 =
Susan	13 − 9 =
Ethan	6 + 7 =
Nadia	8 + 2 =
Dylan	9 + 6 =
Shazia	11 − 6 =
Nina	18 − 9 =
Avi	8 + 8 =
Olivia	17 − 9 =
Liam	7 + 5 =
Thomas	15 − 12 =
Samuel	14 − 8 =
Aisha	6 + 12 =
Lucas	16 − 5 =
Edward	9 + 5 =

Let Freedom Ring

Add. Use the code to write words that tell about America's past.

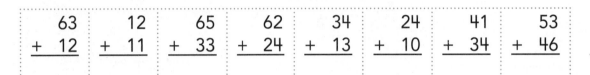

Code

21 Y	23 M	32 T	33 V	34 C	47 I	51 B
64 L	75 A	78 O	86 R	87 U	98 E	99 N

63 + 12	12 + 11	65 + 33	62 + 24	34 + 13	24 + 10	41 + 34	53 + 46
◯	◯	◯	◯	◯	◯	◯	◯

40 + 46	26 + 72	23 + 10	35 + 43	21 + 43	53 + 34	22 + 10	13 + 34	64 + 14	68 + 31
◯	◯	◯	◯	◯	◯	◯	◯	◯	◯

31 + 33	25 + 22	21 + 30	44 + 54	76 + 10	21 + 11	11 + 10
◯	◯	◯	◯	◯	◯	◯

40 + 11	35 + 63	44 + 20	52 + 12
◯	◯	◯	◯

The United States and Canada

Add or subtract.

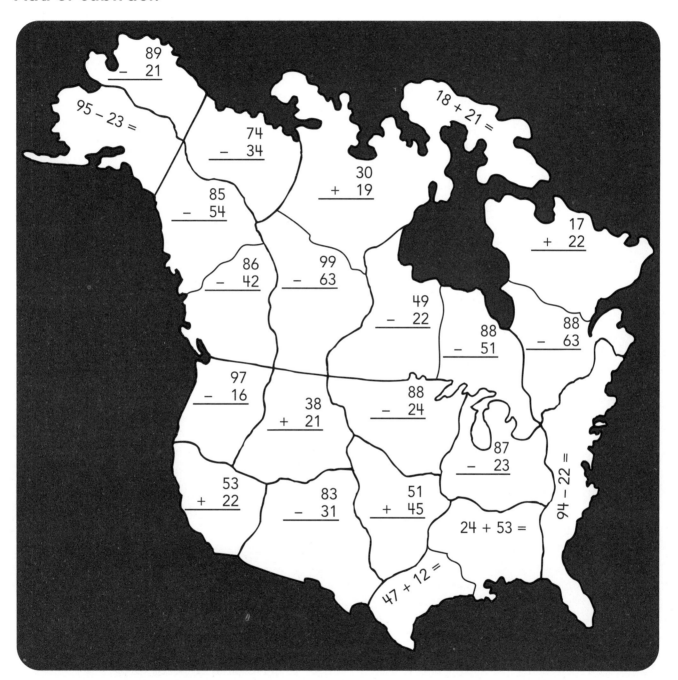

If the answer is between	Color the space
1 and 50	orange (Canada)
51 and 100	blue (United States)

Stars and Stripes

Circle groups of 10. Write the total number of tens and ones.
Write the number in the star.

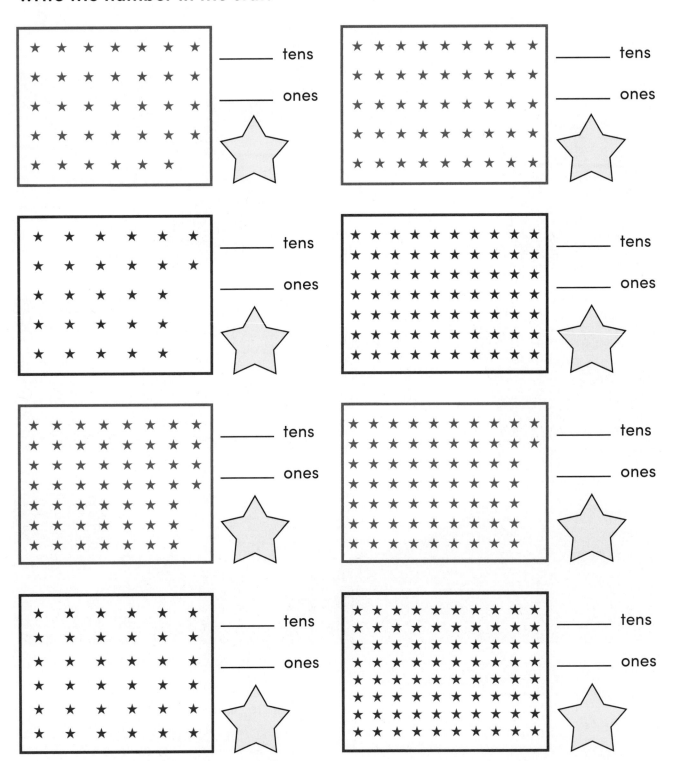

© Scholastic Inc.

The U.S. Capital

Add. Match each building to the correct sum.

Washington Monument	47 + 28
Jefferson Memorial	28 + 35
The White House	27 + 15
Lincoln Memorial	29 + 29
U.S. Capitol Building	39 + 45
Museum of History and Technology	36 + 55

> 68 and < 81

> 50 and < 63

> 40 and < 53

> 87 and < 94

> 59 and < 68

> 82 and < 87

American Presidents

Add. Write the letters in the circles to identify each president.

I was a leader in the Civil War.

39 + 13	38 + 15	56 + 26	26 + 35	29 + 67	27 + 25	43 + 39

◯ ◯ ◯ ◯ ◯ ◯ ◯

I helped write the Declaration of Independence.

19 + 18	28 + 55	24 + 18	19 + 23	17 + 66	59 + 19	49 + 15	78 + 18	48 + 34

◯ ◯ ◯ ◯ ◯ ◯ ◯ ◯ ◯

I was a leader in the American Revolutionary War.

59 + 39	48 + 24	27 + 37	19 + 46	27 + 26	38 + 44	27 + 18	18 + 29	38 + 58	27 + 55

◯ ◯ ◯ ◯ ◯ ◯ ◯ ◯ ◯ ◯

Code

61 **C**	98 **W**	55 **Y**	83 **E**	45 **G**	82 **N**	78 **R**	65 **H**	52 **L**
96 **O**	42 **F**	86 **K**	47 **T**	72 **A**	37 **J**	64 **S**	53 **I**	36 **D**

Time for a Trip!

Look at the number on each form of transportation. Write the number of tens and ones. Regroup. Write the new number.

37
__3__ tens
__7__ ones

Trade 1 ten for 10 ones.

__2__ tens
__17__ ones

52
_____ tens
_____ ones

Trade 1 ten for 10 ones.

_____ tens
_____ ones

85
_____ tens
_____ ones

Trade 1 ten for 10 ones.

_____ tens
_____ ones

43
_____ tens
_____ ones

Trade 1 ten for 10 ones.

_____ tens
_____ ones

68
_____ tens
_____ ones

Trade 1 ten for 10 ones.

_____ tens
_____ ones

26
_____ tens
_____ ones

Trade 1 ten for 10 ones.

_____ tens
_____ ones

Great Vacations

Subtract. Draw a line from each difference to the vacation spot on the map.

Mount Rushmore	Niagara Falls	Gateway Arch	Four Corners Monument	Statue of Liberty
72 − 27	57 − 29	58 − 39	93 − 19	94 − 29

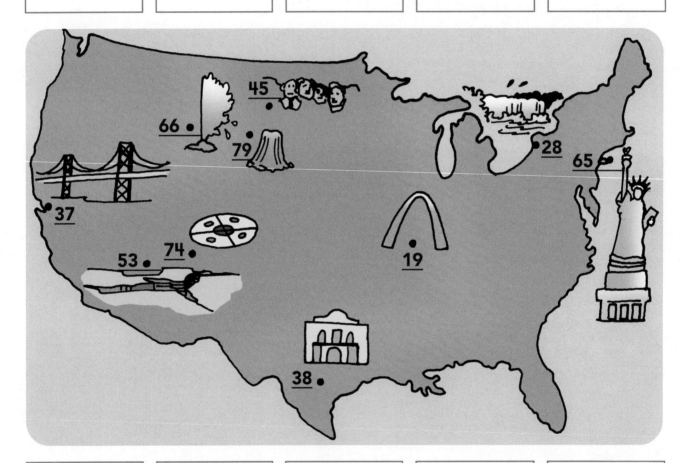

Grand Canyon	Devil's Tower	Golden Gate Bridge	The Alamo	Old Faithful
82 − 29	93 − 14	64 − 27	66 − 28	94 − 28

Weather in the United States

City	High	Low
Anchorage	52°	13°
Chicago	68°	29°
Indianapolis	76°	48°
Newark	68°	39°
Orlando	90°	61°
St. Louis	81°	42°
San Francisco	75°	49°
Seattle	72°	37°

Find the difference between the high and low temperature in each city.

Anchorage	Chicago	Indianapolis	Newark	Orlando	St. Louis	San Francisco	Seattle
52 − 13 — 39							

Find the difference between:

San Francisco high and Chicago low	Orlando high and Anchorage low
Anchorage high and Indianapolis low	St. Louis high and Newark low
Seattle high and San Francisco low	Indianapolis high and Seattle low

Cooling Off

Read each thermometer. Subtract to find the new temperature.

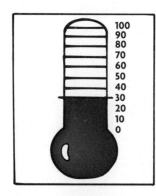 23°

$$
\begin{array}{r}
^{2}\cancel{3}^{10} \\
\cancel{30}° \\
-\ 23° \\
\hline
7°
\end{array}
$$

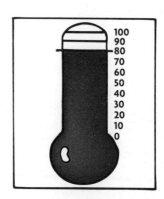 58°

_____
°

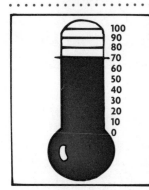 51°

_____
°

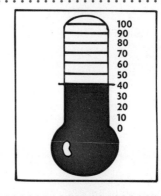 35°

_____
°

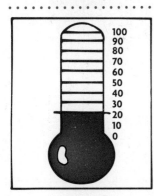 12°

_____
°

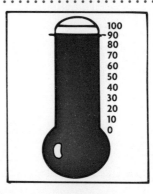 64°

_____
°

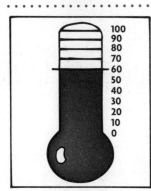 47°

_____
°

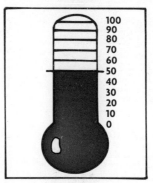 26°

_____
°

America's Favorite Pastime

Add or subtract. Use the chart to color the picture.

white	blue	brown	red	yellow
0–20	21–40	41–60	61–80	81–100

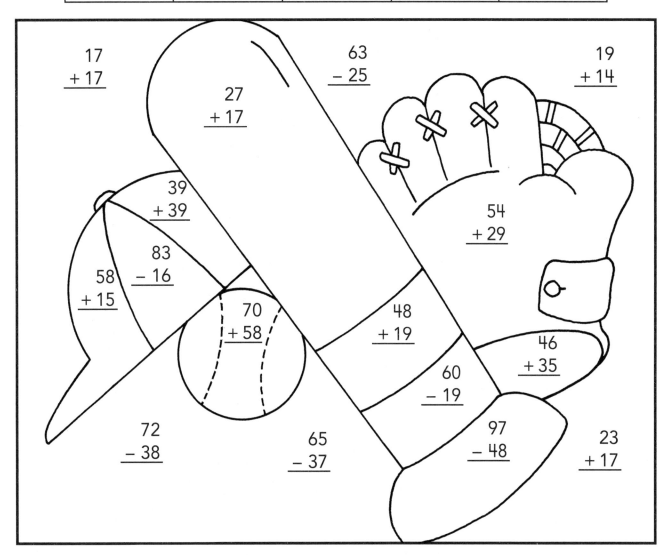

Finish the pattern.

High-Scoring Game

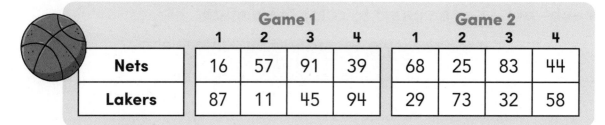

	Game 1				Game 2			
	1	2	3	4	1	2	3	4
Nets	16	57	91	39	68	25	83	44
Lakers	87	11	45	94	29	73	32	58

Look at the scoreboard. Find the total number of baskets in each quarter for each game. Add.

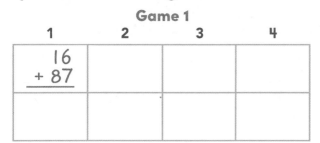

Game 1

1	2	3	4
16 + 87			

Game 2

1	2	3	4

Now, find the difference in baskets in each quarter for each game. Subtract.

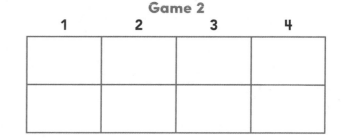

Game 1

1	2	3	4
87 + 16			

Game 2

1	2	3	4

Solve.

1 How many baskets did the Nets score altogether in the first and third quarters of Game 1?

_____ baskets

2 How many more baskets did the Nets score in the third quarter than the second quarter of Game 2?

_____ baskets

3 How many baskets did the Lakers score altogether in the second and third quarters of Game 1?

_____ baskets

4 How many more baskets did the Lakers score in the second quarter than the third quarter of Game 2?

_____ baskets

More Fun Sports

Add or subtract.

91 − 67	48 + 43	92 − 45	70 − 17	63 − 47	38 + 54	29 + 36	80 − 42
skating	football	hockey	volleyball	basketball	soccer	tennis	track

Complete the puzzle with the sport that goes with each answer.

Down

1. 47
2. 53
3. 24
5. 38

Across

3. 92
4. 16
5. 65
6. 91

 Choose your favorite sport from above. On another sheet of paper, write a problem with its same answer. Try to write a problem that includes regrouping.

Skating Shapes

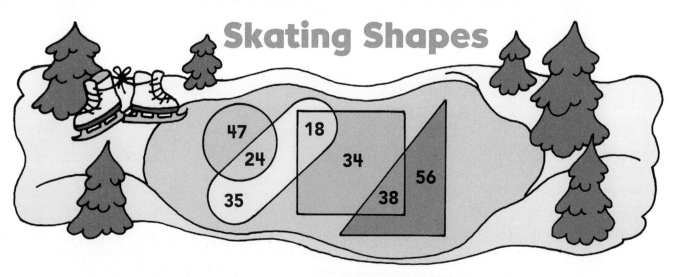

Find the sum of the numbers in each shape above.

$$\begin{array}{r} 56 \\ + 38 \\ \hline \end{array}$$

Use the sums from above to solve.

Find the difference between the greatest number in the ⬤
and the greatest number in the ⬛ .

___ ___

Find the difference between the greatest number in the ◢
and the smallest number in the ⬭ .

___ ___

Great Math Inventions

Add or subtract. Then, write the problem's letter above its matching answer below.

S   29
      + 46

I   48
      − 24

A   27
      + 38

R   56
      − 18

R   37
      + 47

W   81
      − 24

H   23
      + 35

I   90
      − 26

U   52
      − 19

O   37
      + 35

L   70
      − 19

M   82
      − 48

B   23
      + 48

L   52
      + 28

G   91
      − 22

U   73
      − 25

___ ___ ___ ___ ___ ___ ___   ___ ___ ___ ___ ___ ___ ___ ___ ___
57 24 80 51 64 65 34   71 48 84 38 72 33 69 58 75

invented and patented the adding machine in St. Louis, Missouri, in 1888.

It All Adds Up!

Add. Fill in the missing numbers.

```
    3  2  4          2  4 □          □  5  5          2 □  3
  + 6  3 □        + □  5  1        + 3 □  1        + □  1  3
  ──────────      ──────────      ──────────      ──────────
    □ □  6          7 □  2          4  8 □          5  2 □


    4  1 □          □  4  3          2 □ □          □  3  1
  + 3 □  2        + 1  4 □        + 2  1  6        + 4 □ □
  ──────────      ──────────      ──────────      ──────────
    □  3  7          2 □  9          □  1  8          8  5  3


    1 □  2          □  4  1          3  3 □          □  1  2
  + □  3  3        + 1  3 □        + □ □  3        + 2 □  2
  ──────────      ──────────      ──────────      ──────────
    3  7 □          6 □  5          6  6  8          9  4 □


    2  2 □          5 □  4          2  2  4          □  1  6
  + 3  1  4        + □  3  4        + 1 □  3        + 1  3 □
  ──────────      ──────────      ──────────      ──────────
    □ □  4          8  4 □          □  6 □          5 □  8
```

 Joe and Ellie were going to the movies. Joe brought $5.□0, and Ellie brought $□.35. If they had $9.75 altogether, how much money did they each have? Show your work on another sheet of paper.

It's Electrifying!

Regroup tens into hundreds. Draw a line to connect.

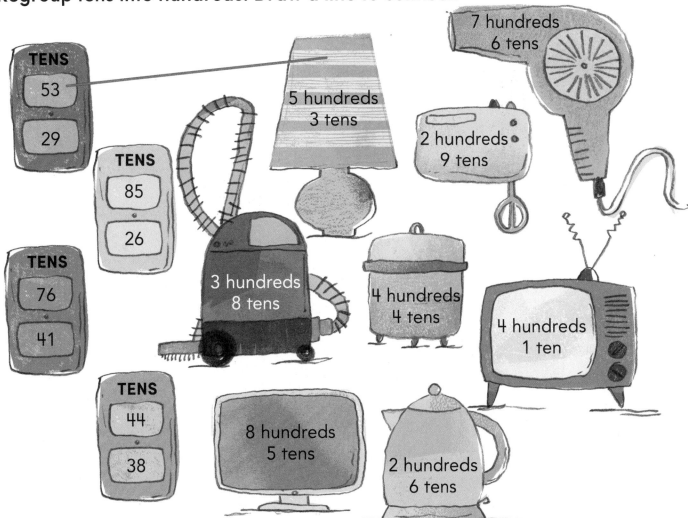

Fill in each missing number.

hundreds	tens	ones	number
200	40	7	2 4 7
400	70	6	___ ___ ___
300		2	___ 9 ___
100	90		___ ___ 3
500		1	___ 6 ___

Scholastic Success With Addition & Subtraction • Grade 3   **23**

Let the Light Shine

Regroup hundreds to tens.

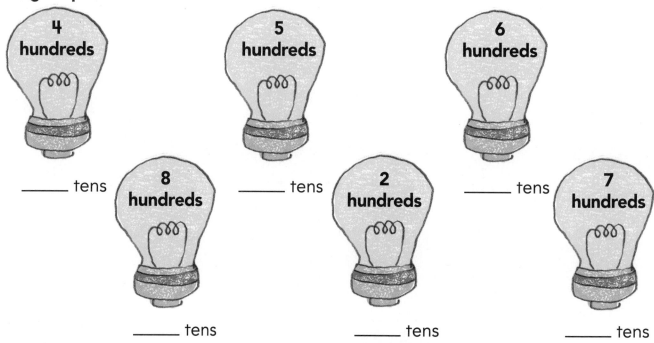

_____ tens

_____ tens

_____ tens

_____ tens

_____ tens

_____ tens

Circle the light bulb in each box with the greater value.

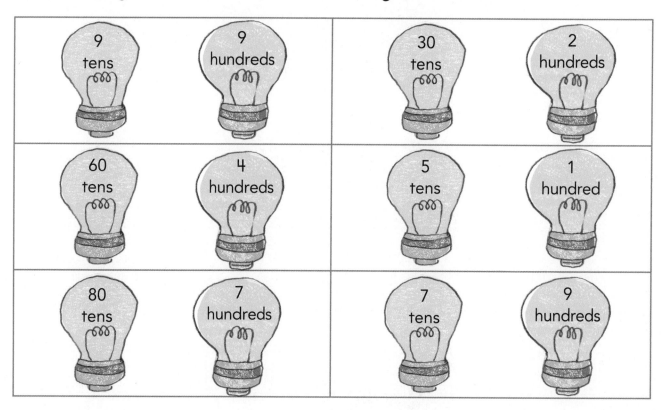

A, B, C . . .

Add.

286 + 668	138 + 289	285 + 269
496 + 188	159 + 190	175 + 189
499 + 446	375 + 469	183 + 289
299 + 158	196 + 378	657 + 285
186 + 287	157 + 267	276 + 566

295 + 675	188 + 185	487 + 385
284 + 439	389 + 188	595 + 289
128 + 379	297 + 179	198 + 199
365 + 378	192 + 579	123 + 589
386 + 189	295 + 379	436 + 538

This letter sounds like a question. Color each answer with a 4 in the ones place to see!

This letter names a feature on your face. Color each answer with a 7 in the tens place to see!

. . . X, Y, and Z

Add.

298 + 276	191 + 343	269 + 289
157 + 189	137 + 369	278 + 485
395 + 457	244 + 279	499 + 446
288 + 664	236 + 288	577 + 388
498 + 399	399 + 164	284 + 439

259 + 467	364 + 258	487 + 436
199 + 128	199 + 89	238 + 287
255 + 373	509 + 315	117 + 304
257 + 569	276 + 566	149 + 279
339 + 385	258 + 467	179 + 348

This letter names a delicious drink.
Color each answer with a 5 in the
hundreds place to see!

This letter names an insect that
stings. Color each answer with
a 2 in the tens place to see!

Number Decoder

Find the number that goes
with each letter in the
problems below.
Then subtract.

J D H – A P L	– _____

G M Q – C S V	– _____

E W A – B Y N	– _____

M A L – F N O	– _____

W T U – J V W	– _____

R E K – D M P	– _____

T J I – E X Q	– _____

K N H – H Z U	– _____

F D X – B G Y	– _____

Find the numbers for your name. Add to find the sum of the numbers.
Write your answer on another sheet of paper.

Out of This World

Subtract. Use the chart to color the picture.

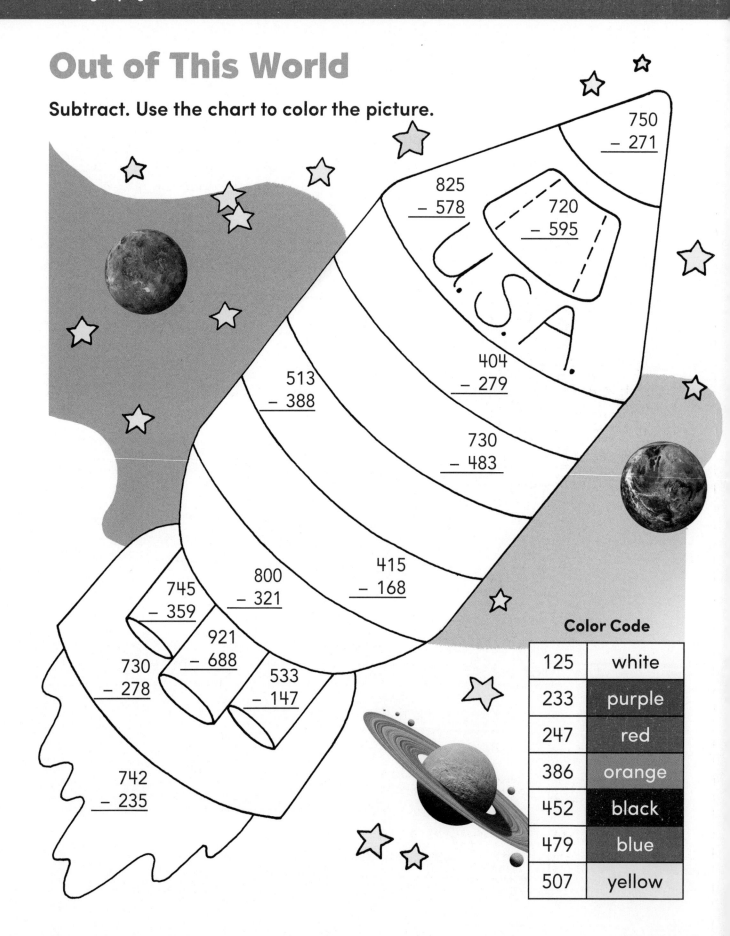

$$750 - 271$$

$$825 - 578$$

$$720 - 595$$

$$404 - 279$$

$$513 - 388$$

$$730 - 483$$

$$415 - 168$$

$$800 - 321$$

$$745 - 359$$

$$921 - 688$$

$$730 - 278$$

$$533 - 147$$

$$742 - 235$$

Color Code

125	white
233	purple
247	red
386	orange
452	black
479	blue
507	yellow

Ride Through the Clouds

Add or subtract.

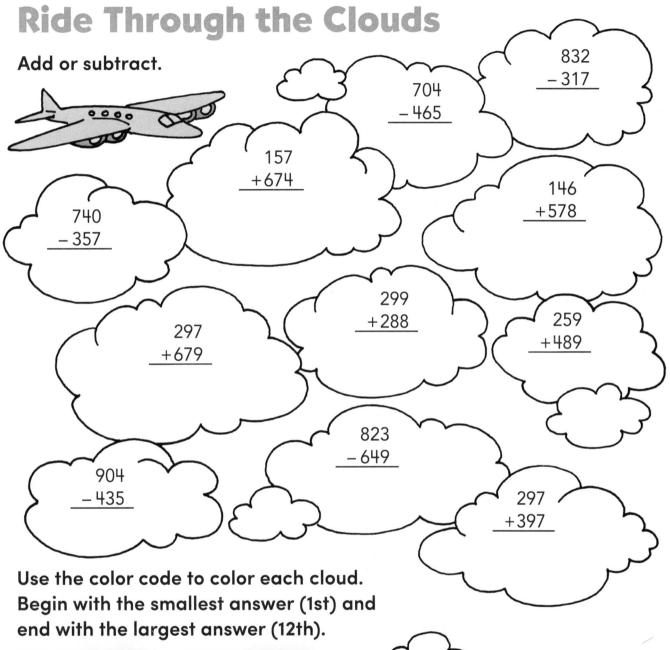

$$\begin{array}{r} 704 \\ -\ 465 \\ \hline \end{array}$$

$$\begin{array}{r} 832 \\ -\ 317 \\ \hline \end{array}$$

$$\begin{array}{r} 157 \\ +\ 674 \\ \hline \end{array}$$

$$\begin{array}{r} 146 \\ +\ 578 \\ \hline \end{array}$$

$$\begin{array}{r} 740 \\ -\ 357 \\ \hline \end{array}$$

$$\begin{array}{r} 299 \\ +\ 288 \\ \hline \end{array}$$

$$\begin{array}{r} 259 \\ +\ 489 \\ \hline \end{array}$$

$$\begin{array}{r} 297 \\ +\ 679 \\ \hline \end{array}$$

$$\begin{array}{r} 823 \\ -\ 649 \\ \hline \end{array}$$

$$\begin{array}{r} 904 \\ -\ 435 \\ \hline \end{array}$$

$$\begin{array}{r} 297 \\ +\ 397 \\ \hline \end{array}$$

**Use the color code to color each cloud.
Begin with the smallest answer (1st) and
end with the largest answer (12th).**

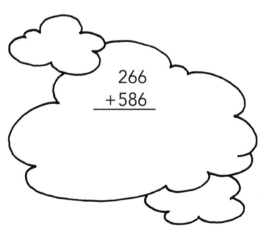

$$\begin{array}{r} 266 \\ +\ 586 \\ \hline \end{array}$$

1st	red		7th	pink
2nd	orange		8th	white
3rd	yellow		9th	black
4th	green		10th	brown
5th	blue		11th	gray
6th	purple		12th	peach

Mailbox Mix-Up

Add or subtract. Match each person to the correct mailbox sum.

My mailbox has a 4, 9, and 3. The 9 is in the ones place.

My mailbox has a 7, 6, and 2. The 2 is in the hundreds place.

My mailbox has a 1, 5, and 5. The 1 is in the ones place.

My mailbox has a 4, 9, and 3. The 9 is in the hundreds place.

My mailbox has a 2, 7, and 6. The 2 is in the ones place.

My mailbox has a 5, 1, and 5. The 1 is in the hundreds place.

My mailbox has a 4, 9, and 3. The 9 is in the tens place.

My mailbox has a 5, 5, and 1. The 1 is in the tens place.

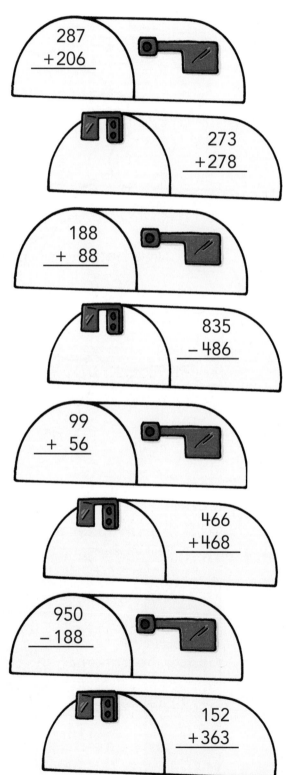

$$287 + 206$$

$$273 + 278$$

$$188 + 88$$

$$835 - 486$$

$$99 + 56$$

$$466 + 468$$

$$950 - 188$$

$$152 + 363$$

Your Part of the World

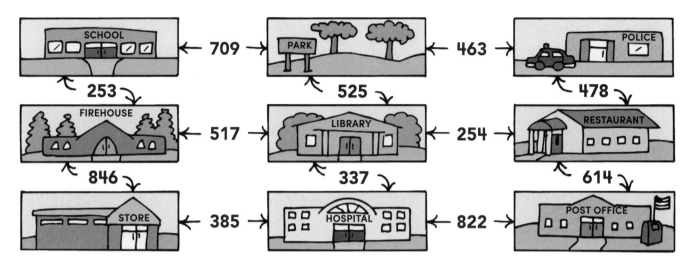

Use the distance between each building to solve each problem.

1. How many feet is it from the firehouse
   to the library to the park? _____

2. How many feet is it from the post office
   to the restaurant to the police station? _____

3. How many feet is it from the park
   to the school to the firehouse? _____

4. Which way is the shortest route—from the
   store to the firehouse to the library or from
   the store to the hospital to the library? Circle.

   $$\begin{array}{r} 846 \\ + 517 \\ \hline \end{array} \qquad \begin{array}{r} 385 \\ + 337 \\ \hline \end{array}$$

5. How much farther is the...

   ...school to the park than the store to the hospital? _____

   ...firehouse to the library than the park to the police station? _____

   ...library to the park than the hospital to the store? _____

Home Sweet Home

Use the coordinates to find each number. Add or subtract.

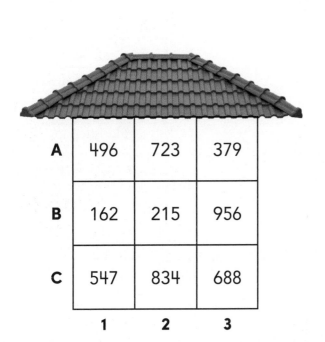

	1	2	3
A	496	723	379
B	162	215	956
C	547	834	688

	4	5	6
E	668	884	345
F	239	716	188
G	422	478	957

1. (A, 1)
   (F, 6) − _____

2. (A, 3)
   (E, 6) + _____

3. (G, 6)
   (C, 3) − _____

4. (B, 3)
   (E, 4) − _____

5. (A, 2)
   (B, 1) − _____

6. (E, 5)
   (C, 2) + _____

7. (C, 1)
   (F, 4) + _____

8. (G, 4)
   (B, 2) − _____

9. (B, 3)
   (G, 5) − _____

 Color the largest number on each house orange. Color the smallest number on each house purple.

What a Beautiful World!

Add or subtract.

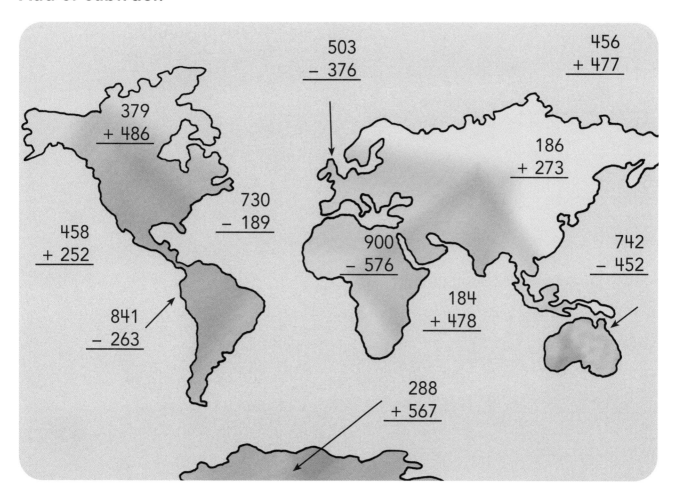

Label the map using the code below.

North America	> 860 and < 927	**Africa**	> 297 and < 334
South America	> 571 and < 658	**Atlantic Ocean**	> 496 and < 560
Australia	> 189 and < 293	**Indian Ocean**	> 581 and < 672
Asia	> 423 and < 538	**Pacific Ocean**	> 671 and < 732
Europe	> 85 and < 266	**Arctic Ocean**	> 867 and < 948
Antarctica	> 748 and < 864		

Majestic Mountains

Add or subtract. Use the code to name four different mountain ranges.

N	6,348
R	8,789
A	5,063
I	7,695
O	2,429
K	5,642
E	7,483
C	3,012
Y	2,351
Z	5,234
L	3,721
U	6,704
P	3,827
S	8,749
D	4,907

```
  2,033      2,411      2,504      4,328
+ 3,030    + 1,310    + 1,323    + 4,421
```

◯   ◯   ◯   ◯

```
  4,258      1,326      1,012      2,321      1,231
+ 4,531    + 1,103    + 2,000    + 3,321    + 1,120
```

◯   ◯   ◯   ◯   ◯

```
  1,204      2,113      2,042      3,746      4,131
+ 1,225    + 3,121    + 3,021    + 5,043    + 1,511
```

◯   ◯   ◯   ◯   ◯

```
  4,053      2,216      2,506      6,471      7,326
+ 1,010    + 4,132    + 2,401    + 1,012    + 1,423
```

◯   ◯   ◯   ◯   ◯

Reach for the Top

Add. Then, starting at the bottom row, add the digits in each sum.
If the digits total 9, color the box to find your way to the top!

$$1,021 + 1,031$$

$$3,432 + 1,154 \qquad 2,130 + 1,200$$

$$1,423 + 1,322 \qquad 2,423 + 1,520 \qquad 4,000 + 4,010$$

$$4,024 + 3,012 \qquad 5,010 + 1,011 \qquad 3,011 + 4,000 \qquad 2,240 + 1,232$$

$$1,412 + 1,351 \qquad 4,201 + 1,100 \qquad 2,431 + 3,132 \qquad 4,631 + 3,210 \qquad 4,302 + 5,502$$

$$3,243 + 4,200 \qquad 2,031 + 1,200 \qquad 4,084 + 2,011 \qquad 1,362 + 1,202 \qquad 3,025 + 1,312 \qquad 6,434 + 3,251$$

One in a Thousand

Add. Write the letters on the lines below in order from the smallest to the largest sums to find out whose face is on the hundred-dollar bill.

F $27.41
+ $12.55

N $59.63
+ $20.33

N $85.42
+ $14.06

R $31.75
+ $35.24

K $64.84
+ $22.15

A $29.35
+ $50.42

L $46.96
+ $42.03

I $73.57
+ $23.43

___ ___ ___ ___ ___ ___ ___ ___

Calculate and write answers on the lines.

If you have 50 hundred-dollar bills, you have _____ thousand dollars!

If you have 20 hundred-dollar bills, you have _____ thousand dollars!

If you have 80 hundred-dollar bills, you have _____ thousand dollars!

If you have 10 hundred-dollar bills, you have _____ thousand dollars!

If you have 30 hundred-dollar bills, you have _____ thousand dollars!

If you have 70 hundred-dollar bills, you have _____ thousand dollars!

If you have 90 hundred-dollar bills, you have _____ thousand dollars!

If you have 40 hundred-dollar bills, you have _____ thousand dollars!

Did You Know?

Add or subtract. Write the letter for the matching number below to find out whose face is on the $50 bill.

(S) $27.99
+ $63.84

(L) $25.59
+ $44.96

(R) $71.90
− $59.17

(E) $13.88
+ $28.08

(S) $80.31
− $46.16

(S) $25.79
+ $38.51

(T) $53.97
− $29.09

(Y) $27.66
+ $43.74

(N) $32.48
+ $17.77

(S) $94.33
− $56.34

(U) $13.88
+ $18.88

(G) $68.74
− $55.29

(A) $63.89
+ $26.53

___ ___ ___ ___ ___ ___ ___
$32.76 $70.55 $71.40 $64.30 $91.83 $41.96 $37.99

___ .   ___ ___ ___ ___ ___
$34.15 $13.45 $12.73 $90.42 $50.25 $24.88

Great Beginnings

Add. Look at each sum. Use the code below to color the picture.

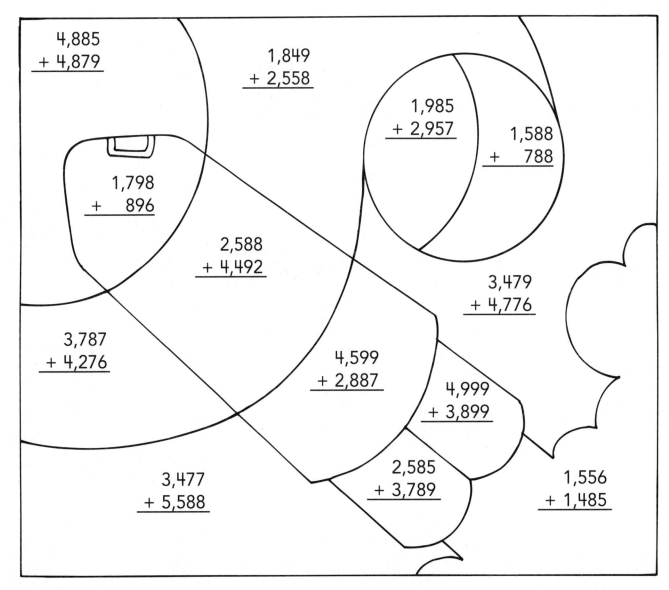

4,885
+ 4,879

1,849
+ 2,558

1,985
+ 2,957

1,588
+   788

1,798
+   896

2,588
+ 4,492

3,479
+ 4,776

3,787
+ 4,276

4,599
+ 2,887

4,999
+ 3,899

3,477
+ 5,588

2,585
+ 3,789

1,556
+ 1,485

4,942 — **blue**   8,063 — **blue**   3,041 — **red**   9,065 — **blue**

2,694 — white   7,486 — white   4,407 — **blue**   9,764 — **orange**

8,898 — **black**   6,374 — **black**   2,376 — yellow   8,255 — **blue**

7,080 — white

Find the year humans first walked on the moon. Add that number to the
year it is now. Use another sheet of paper to do your work.

Styles Change

Add. Match the sums to show the hats and shoes that go together.

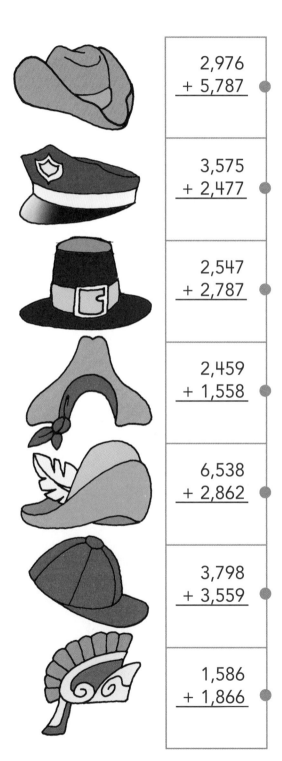

2,976 + 5,787
3,575 + 2,477
2,547 + 2,787
2,459 + 1,558
6,538 + 2,862
3,798 + 3,559
1,586 + 1,866

2,386 + 3,666
1,278 + 2,739
2,645 + 4,712
3,885 + 4,878
1,665 + 1,787
3,655 + 1,679
2,766 + 6,634

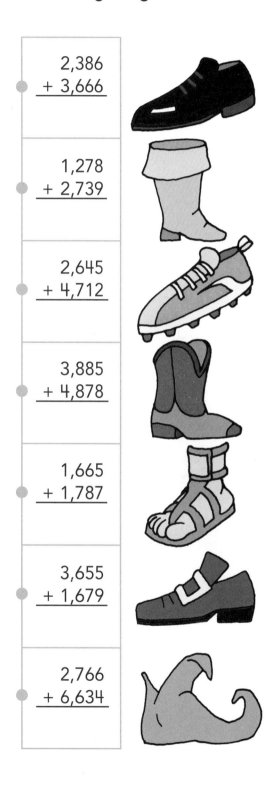

Dynamite Dominoes

Use the same color to color the connecting squares that equal the same amount. Remember, 1 thousand equals 10 hundreds.

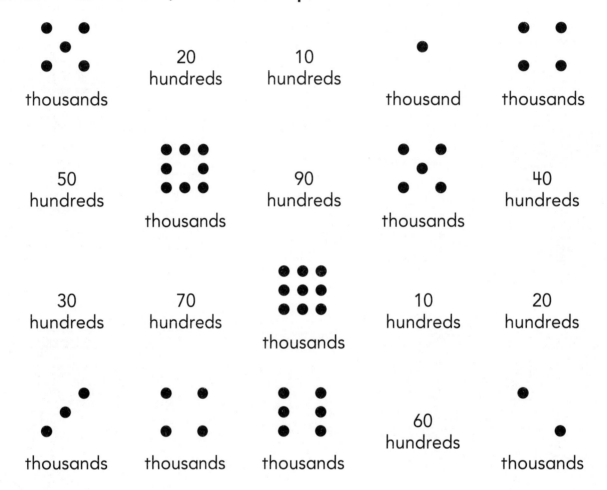

Add. Write the number.

thousands		hundreds		tens		ones		
3	+	1	+	6	+	7	=	
5	+	7	+	0	+	3	=	
6	+	0	+	3	+	9	=	
4	+	5	+	8	+	4	=	
9	+	9	+	4	+	0	=	

Pictures in the Sky

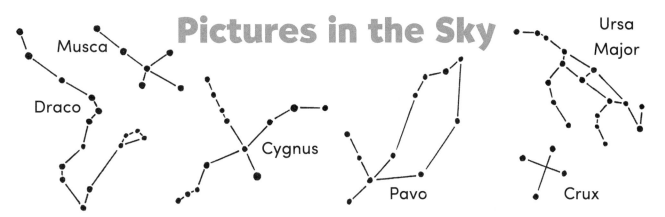

Subtract. Draw a line between matching sums to connect the Latin and English names for each constellation.

Latin		English	
Draco	7,621 − 5,586	8,533 − 2,074	Swan
Pavo	7,340 − 3,758	7,662 − 2,678	Cross
Cygnus	9,317 − 2,858	8,403 − 6,368	Dragon
Ursa Major	8,332 − 3,579	6,441 − 2,859	Peacock
Musca	7,015 − 1,739	7,031 − 2,278	Great Bear
Crux	8,150 − 3,166	8,133 − 2,857	Fly

Imaginary Lines

Subtract.

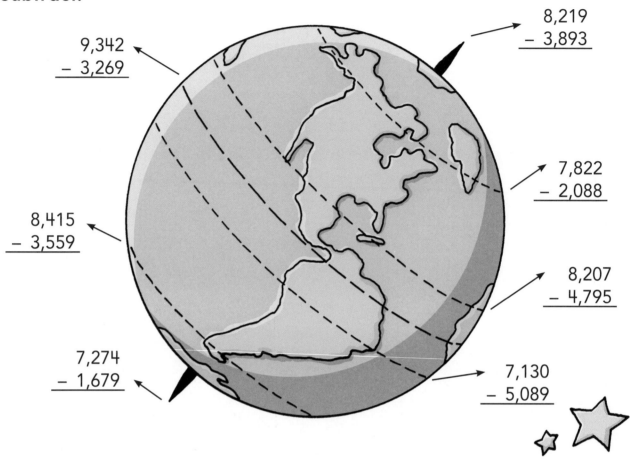

$$\begin{array}{r} 8{,}219 \\ -\ 3{,}893 \\ \hline \end{array}$$

$$\begin{array}{r} 9{,}342 \\ -\ 3{,}269 \\ \hline \end{array}$$

$$\begin{array}{r} 7{,}822 \\ -\ 2{,}088 \\ \hline \end{array}$$

$$\begin{array}{r} 8{,}415 \\ -\ 3{,}559 \\ \hline \end{array}$$

$$\begin{array}{r} 8{,}207 \\ -\ 4{,}795 \\ \hline \end{array}$$

$$\begin{array}{r} 7{,}274 \\ -\ 1{,}679 \\ \hline \end{array}$$

$$\begin{array}{r} 7{,}130 \\ -\ 5{,}089 \\ \hline \end{array}$$

Find the sum of the digits in each answer to identify each global marking. Label them.

7	Tropic of Capricorn
10	Tropic of Cancer
15	North Pole
16	Equator
19	Arctic Circle
23	Antarctic Circle
24	South Pole

Long, Long Ago

Add or subtract. Use the chart to color the picture.

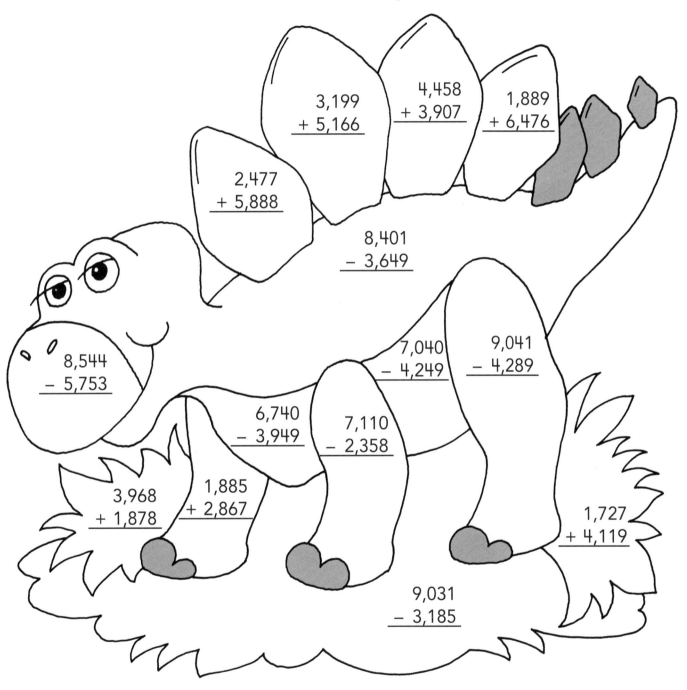

green	brown	yellow	pink
5,846	**4,752**	**8,365**	**2,791**

Fun With Numbers

Add or subtract. Then, write the problem's
letter above its matching answer below.

W   2,376
  + 2,784

O   8,500
  − 2,763

T   4,401
  − 2,550

A   2,763
  + 3,857

H   8,455
  − 1,867

!   4,672
  + 3,885

E   6,345
  − 2,660

M   8,304
  − 2,541

M   2,463
  + 4,908

E   4,365
  − 1,478

A   1,074
  + 5,988

S   3,453
  + 2,778

___ ___ ___ ___   is   ___ ___ ___ ___ ___ ___ ___ ___
5,763 7,062 1,851 6,588   6,620 5,160 2,887 6,231 5,737 7,371 3,685 8,557

© Scholastic Inc.

Classy Animals

In the 1700s, a Swedish botanist devised a system for classifying plants and animals. The system's basic design is still being used today. To learn the botanist's name, add or subtract each problem.

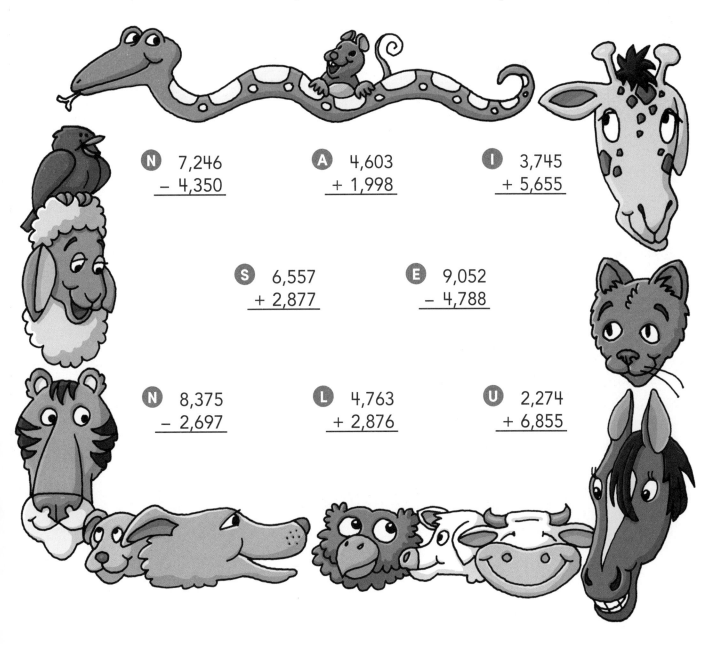

N 7,246
− 4,350

A 4,603
+ 1,998

I 3,745
+ 5,655

S 6,557
+ 2,877

E 9,052
− 4,788

N 8,375
− 2,697

L 4,763
+ 2,876

U 2,274
+ 6,855

Carolus _____ _____ _____ _____ _____ _____ _____ _____
  7,639 9,400 2,896 5,678 6,601 4,264 9,129 9,434

ANSWER KEY

Page 5
18, 7, 15; 18, 16, 14; 18, 15, 17;
8, 18, 15; 18, 9, 15; 12, 9, 18;
16, 11, 17; 13, 11, 18; 4, 9, 2; 14, 18, 16

Page 6
14, 8, 2, 5, 11, spade
2, 7, 11, axe
4, 2, 5, 1, 17, radio
14, 2, 10, 11, 4, saber
Put an X on the radio.

Page 7
7, 4, 13, 10, 15, 5, 9, 16, 8, 12, 3,
6, 18, 11, 14
Aisha, Avi, Dylan, Edward, Ethan,
Liam, Lucas, Nadia, Nina, Olivia, Pari,
Sam, Shazia, Susan, Thomas

Page 8
75, 23, 98, 86, 47, 34, 75, 99,
AMERICAN
86, 98, 33, 78, 64, 87, 32, 47, 78, 99,
REVOLUTION
64, 47, 51, 98, 86, 32, 21,
LIBERTY
51, 98, 64, 64,
BELL

Page 9

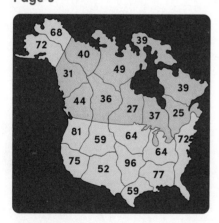

Page 10
Check that each student has circled
the correct number of stars.

3 tens, 4 ones, 34	4 tens, 5 ones, 45
2 tens, 7 ones, 27	7 tens, 0 ones, 70
5 tens, 3 ones, 53	6 tens, 5 ones, 65
3 tens, 6 ones, 36	8 tens, 0 ones, 80

Page 11

Washington Monument — **75**
Jefferson Memorial — **63**
The White House — **42**
Lincoln Memorial — **58**
U.S. Capitol Building — **84**
Museum of History and Technology — **91**

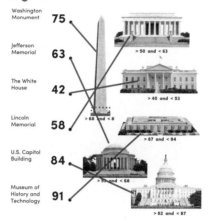

> 50 and < 63
> 40 and < 53
> 68 and < 8
> 87 and < 94
> 53 and < 68
> 82 and < 87

Page 12
52, 53, 82, 61, 96, 52, 82,
LINCOLN
37, 83, 42, 42, 83, 78, 64, 96, 82,
JEFFERSON
98, 72, 64, 65, 53, 82, 45, 47, 96, 82,
WASHINGTON

Page 13
37: 3 tens 7 ones, 2 tens 17 ones
52: 5 tens 2 ones, 4 tens 12 ones
85: 8 tens 5 ones, 7 tens 15 ones
43: 4 tens 3 ones, 3 tens 13 ones
68: 6 tens 8 ones, 5 tens 18 ones
26: 2 tens 6 ones, 1 ten 16 ones

Page 14

Mount Rushmore	Niagara Falls	Gateway Arch	Four Corners Monument	Statue of Liberty
45	28	19	74	65

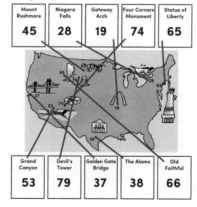

Grand Canyon	Devil's Tower	Golden Gate Bridge	The Alamo	Old Faithful
53	79	37	38	66

Page 15
52 – 13 = 39, 68 – 29 = 39,
76 – 48 = 28, 68 – 39 = 29,
90 – 61 = 29, 81 – 42 = 39,
75 – 49 = 26, 72 – 37 = 35,
75 – 29 = 46, 90 – 13 = 77,
52 – 48 = 4, 81 – 39 = 42,
72 – 49 = 23, 76 – 37 = 39

Page 16
30 – 23 = 7, 80 – 58 = 22,
70 – 51 = 19, 40 – 35 = 5,
20 – 12 = 8, 90 – 64 = 26,
60 – 47 = 13, 50 – 26 = 24

Page 17

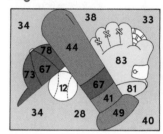

32, 34, 36, 38, 40, 42, 44, 46, 48, 50

Page 18
Game 1: 16 + 87 = 103, 57 + 11 = 68,
91 + 45 = 136, 39 + 49 = 133
Game 2: 68 + 29 = 97, 25 + 73 = 98,
83 + 32 = 115, 44 + 58 = 102
Game 1: 87 – 16 = 71, 57 – 11 = 46,
91 – 45 = 46, 94 – 39 = 55
Game 2: 68 – 29 = 39, 73 – 25 = 48,
83 – 32 = 51, 58 – 44 = 14
1. 107 **2.** 58 **3.** 139 **4.** 41

Page 19
24, 91, 47, 53, 16, 92, 65, 38

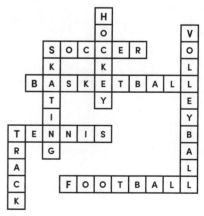

Page 20
56 + 38 = 94, 18 + 24 + 35 = 77,
38 + 34 + 18 = 90, 47 + 24 = 71;
90 − 77 = 13, 94 − 77 = 17,
90 − 71 = 19, 94 − 71 = 23;
47 − 38 = 9, 56 − 18 = 38

Page 21
S. 75 **I.** 24 **A.** 65 **R.** 38 **R.** 84 **W.** 57
H. 58 **I.** 64 **U.** 33 **O.** 72 **L.** 51 **M.** 34
B. 71 **L.** 80 **G.** 69 **U.** 48;
WILLIAM BURROUGHS

Page 22
324 + 632 = 956, 241 + 551 = 792,
155 + 331 = 486, 213 + 313 = 526,
415 + 322 = 737, 143 + 146 = 289,
202 + 216 = 418, 431 + 422 = 853,
142 + 233 = 375, 541 + 134 = 675,
335 + 333 = 668, 712 + 232 = 944,
220 + 314 = 534, 514 + 334 = 848,
224 + 143 = 367, 416 + 132 = 548;
Extra Activity: Joe brought $5.40,
and Ellie brought $4.35.

Page 23

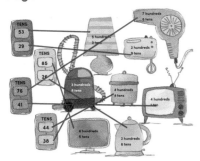

200, 40, 7, 247; 400, 70, 6, 476;
300, 90, 2, 392; 100, 90, 3, 193;
500, 60, 1, 561

Page 24
40, 50, 60, 80, 20, 70; 9 hundreds,
30 tens, 60 tens, 1 hundred,
80 tens, 9 hundreds

Page 25

954	427	554		970	373	872
684	349	364		723	577	884
945	844	472		507	476	397
457	574	942		743	771	712
473	424	842		575	674	974

Page 26

574	534	558		726	622	923
346	506	763		327	288	525
852	523	945		628	824	421
952	524	965		826	842	428
897	563	723		724	725	527

Page 27
534 − 275 = 259, 467 − 278 = 189,
392 − 296 = 96, 625 − 366 = 259,
988 − 589 = 399, 735 − 367 = 368,
854 − 397 = 457, 564 − 498 = 66,
339 − 249 = 90

Page 28

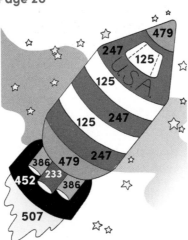

Page 29

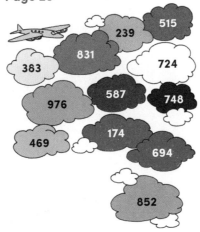

Page 30

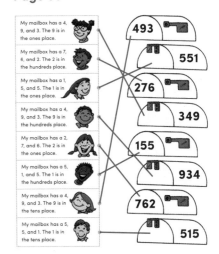

Page 31
1. 517 + 525 = 1,042 **2.** 614 + 478 = 1,092
3. 709 + 253 = 962 **4.** 1,363, (722)
5. 709 − 385 = 324, 517 − 463 = 54,
525 − 385 = 140

Page 32
1. 496 − 188 = 308
2. 379 + 345 = 724
3. 957 − 688 = 269
4. 956 − 668 = 288
5. 723 − 162 = 561
6. 884 + 834 = 1,718
7. 547 + 239 = 786
8. 422 − 215 = 207
9. 956 − 478 = 478
Extra Activity: Check coloring.

Page 33

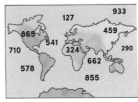

Check labeling.

Page 34
5,063, 3,721, 3,827, 8,749, **ALPS**
8,789, 2,429, 3,012, 5,642, 2,351,
ROCKY
2,429, 5,234, 5,063, 8,789, 5,642,
OZARK
5,063, 6,348, 4,907, 7,483, 8,749,
ANDES

Page 35

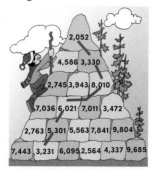

2,052
4,586 3,330
2,745 3,943 8,010
7,036 6,021 7,011 3,472
2,763 5,301 5,563 7,841 9,804
7,443 3,231 6,095 2,564 4,337 9,685

Page 36

F. $39.96 N. $79.96 N. $99.48
R. $66.99 K. $86.99 A. $79.77
L. $88.99 I. $97.00
FRANKLIN
5, 2, 8, 1, 3, 7, 9, 4

Page 37

S. $91.83 L. $70.55 R. $12.73
E. $41.96 S. $34.15 S. $64.30
T. $24.88 Y. $71.40 N. $50.25
S. $37.99 U. $32.76 G. $13.45
A. $90.42
ULYSSES S. GRANT

Page 38

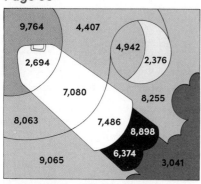

9,764   4,407
4,942
2,694   2,376
7,080
8,255
8,063   7,486
8,898
6,374
9,065   3,041

Extra Activity: Answers will vary.

Page 39

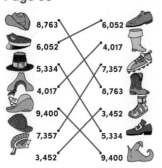

8,763   6,052
6,052   4,017
5,334   7,357
4,017   8,763
9,400   3,452
7,357   5,334
3,452   9,400

Page 40

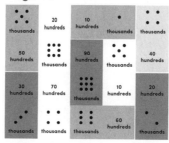

20 thousands	20 hundreds	10 hundreds	thousands	thousands
50 hundreds	thousands	90 hundreds	thousands	40 hundreds
30 hundreds	70 hundreds	thousands	10 hundreds	20 hundreds
thousands	thousands	thousands	60 hundreds	thousands

3,167, 5,703, 6,039, 4,584, 9,940

Page 41

Latin		English
Draco	2,035	6,459 Swan
Pavo	3,582	4,984 Cross
Cygnus	6,459	2,035 Dragon
Ursa Major	4,753	3,582 Peacock
Musca	5,276	4,753 Great Bear
Crux	4,984	5,276 Fly

Page 42

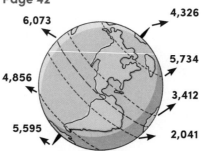

6,073   4,326
5,734
4,856
3,412
5,595   2,041

Check labeling.

Page 43

8,365 8,365 8,365
8,365
4,752
2,791 2,791 4,752
2,791
4,752
5,846 4,752   5,846
5,846

Page 44

5,160 5,737 1,851
6,620
3,685 6,588 8,557
5,763
7,371
7,062 2,887
6,231

MATH is AWESOME!

Page 45

N. 2,896 A. 6,601 I. 9,400
S. 9,434 E. 4,264 N. 5,678
L. 7,639 U. 9,129
Carolus LINNAEUS